FIGURES
& FACES

PATRICK MAURIÈS AND ÉVELYNE POSSÉMÉ

FIGURES & FACES

THE ART OF JEWELRY

Photographs
Jean-Marie del Moral

pp. 6–7
Maison Morel et Cie
Châtelaine
Paris, 1842–48
Silver, partially gilded silver, gold, enamel
L. 27 cm; W. 7 cm
Gift of the Marquis de Nadaillac, 1920
Inv. 21779

p. 10
Ernest Hue, sculptor
Cupid Bound to Reason brooch
Paris, Salon of 1861
After a drawing by Pierre-Paul Prud'hon
presented at the Salon of 1793, executed
as an engraving by Jacques-Louis Copia
in the same year
Coloured gold, onyx cameo, rose-cut
diamonds mounted on silver
H. 4.2 cm; W 4.1 cm
Gift of Henri Vever, 1924
Inv. 24440

pp. 16–17
Alphonse Fouquet (1828–1911), jeweler
Albert-Ernest Carrier-Belleuse (1824–87),
sculptor
Honoré Bourdoncle, known as Honoré,
engraver
Paul Grandhomme (1851–1944), enameller
Diana bracelet
Paris, 1883
Coloured gold, enamel painted on gold,
rose-cut diamonds mounted on silver
H. 8 cm; L. 18 cm
Gift of Alphonse Fouquet, 1908
Inv. 14851 A

p. 18
René Lalique (1860–1945)
Brooch
Paris, c. 1898–99
Gold, enamel on gold, pearl, limestone
H. 6.2 cm; W. 4.5 cm
Bequest of Marquise Arconati-Visconti
in memory of M. Raoul Duseigneur, 1916
Inv. 20371

p. 24
Ring with miniature
France (?), late 18th century
Gilded silver, miniature on ivory,
paste gemstones
H. 3.7 cm; Diam. 2 cm; W. 2.5 cm
Gift of Mme Délicourt in memory
of her brother, M. Thierry, 1937
Inv. 33604

p. 25
Child, Doves and Dog ring
France (?), 18th century
Silver, gold, coloured white onyx,
rock crystal
H. 2.7 cm; W. 1.8 cm
Gift of Cérette Meyer in memory
of her brother, 1914
Inv. 19437

Gift of Friendship ring
France, late 18th century
Gold, enamel on guilloché enamel
ground, white coral, mother-of-pearl,
rock crystal
H. 2.5 cm; W. 1.5 cm; Diam. 1.7 cm
Bequest of Jean Jacques Reubell, 1934
Inv. 31039

CONTENTS

The publication of Figures & Faces completes a trilogy devoted to the jewelry collection of the Musée des Arts Décoratifs in Paris, one of the finest treasure troves of its kind in the world. While the two previous volumes in the series explored the rich but relatively well-known subjects of Flora and Fauna, this book takes as its theme another, more intimate, aspect of the history of jewelry-making, one that often invokes connections with famous figures. In these pages, we will find Marie-Antoinette and Alberto Giacometti, the vanitas collection of Baroness Henri de Rothschild, glittering lips by Claude Lalanne and Solange Azagury-Partridge and an intently gazing eye, an 18th-century miniature set in a pendant. From one era to the next, the beauty of female bodies takes centre stage.

This clearly defined subject becomes the launching point for a joyous trip through the eclectic collections of the Musée des Arts Décoratifs. The figures and faces themselves are key to fully understanding this spiritual and poetic journey: devotional objects adorned with religious scenes, mythological marvels, faces that echo the motifs of Symbolism, portraits of Renaissance heroines, Art Nouveau nymphs and Cubist goddesses. The chosen objects also serve as a worthy tribute to our donors, whose names include some of the greatest jewelry designers: Jean Jacques Reubell, Baroness Henri de Rothschild, Henri Vever, Alphonse Fouquet, the Marquise Arconati-Visconti, and my respected predecessor Yvonne Brunhammer.

This trilogy could not have been completed without Évelyne Possémé and Patrick Mauriès, who once more supply their own special combination of scholarly understanding and original thinking, enhanced by the photographic talents of Jean-Marie del Moral. Nor would this book have been possible without the generous support of the École des Arts Joailliers and the jewelry house of Van Cleef & Arpels. Yet again, it is a pleasure to thank Marie Vallanet and Nicolas Bos for their trust and kindness in helping us to showcase this exceptional museum collection, by means of an extraordinary partnership between heritage and creativity.

Olivier Gabet
Director of the Musée des Arts Décoratifs

ollowing the publication of Flora and Fauna, *dedicated to the extraordinary jewelry collection of the Musée des Arts Décoratifs in Paris, the École des Arts Joailliers is delighted to introduce* Figures & Faces, *the third and final book in this series. Erudite and educational, these books showcase the history of jewelry through three universal themes, reflecting the primary functions of adornment over the centuries: initiation and protection, pageantry and emotional expression.*

These striking pieces are presented at their multifaceted best, away from display cases and protective glass. The eye can appreciate every tiny detail, admiring the glitter of precious metals, the clarity and depth of gemstones, the texture of a cameo or the delicacy of a carving. Whether inspired by flora, fauna, or human figures and faces, the deeper significance of the motifs is brought to the fore in works by both anonymous masters and the great names of jewelry design.

As patron of the museum's jewelry gallery since 2015, the École des Arts Joailliers has been honoured to support the publication of this trilogy of books, allowing readers to share the richness and splendour of jewelry past and present. Founded in 2012 with the support of Van Cleef & Arpels, the school of jewelry arts allows the public to discover the craft and history of jewelry-making and gemmology through a range of different courses, workshops, lectures, exhibitions and publications, both in Paris and around the world. Its enduring partnership with the Musée des Arts Décoratifs is testimony to the shared values that guide the actions of both institutions: a desire to educate and to pass on knowledge and culture.

Marie Vallanet
President, École des Arts Joailliers

Nicolas Bos
President, Van Cleef & Arpels

DISCREET EFFIGIES

O f the three decorative themes selected for this trilogy of books – *Flora* and *Fauna* followed by *Figures & Faces* – the third is surely the most emotionally charged because it makes us engage with our own image; it represents our most superficial, most immediate reality and yet at the same time it evokes a deep sense of intimacy. The depiction of the human figure is associated with the cardinal virtues and passions of humanity: memory, faith, affection, love, separation, loss, mourning.

In miniature form, figurative jewelry, even at its most formulaic, always retains something of the singularity and uniqueness of a painted or engraved portrait, of which it may be regarded as a particular subtype. Yet it is substantially different in that it does not demand the distance and space needed in order to read a picture – on the contrary, it suggests proximity, contiguity, emotional involvement, and because it is worn next to the skin, a form of contact that reflects its emotive nature.

Whatever form it takes (commemorative, religious, romantic), figurative jewelry always seeks to hold and retain the trace of a presence, somehow concentrating and crystallizing it in as dense a form as possible, creating a kind of diamond made of memories. The human figure differs from other motifs, such as flora and fauna, in that it lends itself less easily to stylization (let alone abstraction) than to categorization, whether in terms of uniqueness (personal or historical) or idealization (religious and mythological). More so than other subjects, figurative motifs express a tension between the generic (in the case of divine or heroic images) and the specific (an object of love or mourning), with the chosen form depending on the nature or purpose of the jewelry.

Historians believe that the love of portrait miniatures that grew from the Renaissance onwards was part of a rediscovery of the classical world. This revival was somewhat paradoxical, since there are no surviving examples of paintings, let alone portraits, from antiquity, other than wall-paintings and the much later Fayum mummy portraits. Similarly, most works of sculpture from antiquity, with the exception, in this case, of tomb sculptures, provide only highly idealized images.

Medallions and cameos were in fact the main sources for this resurgence, whose origin is traced by Diana Scarisbrick (*Portrait Jewels,* 2011) to the small Italian courts of Isabella d'Este and the Borgias. It was there that portrait medals, cast in small numbers, served both to disseminate and to promote the image of a princely ruler, while cameos, as unique works, were more direct symbols of patronage or marks of favour; a later, curious neoclassical pendant from the collections of the Musée des Arts Décoratifs is a rare, hybrid example of these two forms (p. 80).

The portrait miniature saw a remarkable flowering in 16th-century Europe. The Valois, Tudors and Habsburgs commissioned works from great artists – including François Clouet and Nicholas Hilliard – who were also virtuoso miniaturists. Elizabeth I's skilful promotion of her own myth, together with the flourishing of English miniatures, led to the creation of small masterpieces. In France, Louis XIV turned these small but highly diverse objects into a key tool for disseminating his image. And when Napoleon in his turn sought to formulate a style for his own reign, he did so by reviving the use of the cameo as a symbol of continuity with the classical world, which had been granted a new topicality by the excavation of the ruins of Herculaneum and Pompeii.

Although portraiture was used for political purposes, in the broadest sense, that did not preclude it from having an emotional or intimate dimension, which gradually grew stronger with the changing sensibilities and rise of the bourgeoisie in the 18th century. As a personal possession, jewelry became primarily a form of declaration, even when it was encoded and disguised as in the case of images of fallen sovereigns – Charles I, Louis XVI and Marie-Antoinette – who had fallen from public grace but whose portraits people would keep, concealed in a locket, as close as possible to their person, as a secret symbol of allegiance.

This dialectic between what is shown and what is concealed also applies to jewelry's emotional connections: to family relationships (such as the striking cameo bracelet carved by James Pradier with a portrait of his three children, see pp. 92–93) and the ties of love, but also to their darker side: separation or loss. Yale University possesses a charming example of an invisible declaration of love. It is a locket featuring a self-portrait by Nathaniel Hancock, a miniaturist about whom little is known, except that he was working in America at the time of the Revolution, a period when, as few now realize, figurative jewelry was flourishing. The locket opens to reveal a heart playing-card, a secret token of his love for his wife (*Love and Loss* exhibition catalogue, 2001).

Then there is the famous ring in which Madame du Châtelet reverently kept an image of her current favourite, and which gave rise to a pointed remark by Voltaire, recorded by Madame de Graffigny. As he was examining the Marquise's ring, the bezel fell open by mistake and revealed the face of Saint-Lambert, whereupon Voltaire exclaimed: 'Oh! Just like a woman!... After all, I had seen off the Duc de Richelieu, then Saint-Lambert saw me off, and so one takes over where the other leaves off.' (*Vie privée de Voltaire et Madame du Châtelet,* 1820).

Whether overt or concealed, the declarative quality of figurative jewelry is never a laughing matter – it is a form of commitment, however fleeting (as in the case of Madame du Châtelet). That is why Araminte replies to Dorante in Marivaux's play *Les Fausses Confidences* (1737): 'Give you my portrait! Don't you realize that would mean admitting that I love you?' And this admission can be underlined by a range of motifs discreetly added to cases and mounts, silent symbols scattered around the face of the beloved to affirm the unique and intense nature of the declaration. Some are easy to decipher (like the Greek letter *phi,* for fidelity). Others, although once in common use, might easily pass unnoticed today; few now know the meaning of the *fermesse,* a letter S with a diagonal stroke through it, a symbol of love, constancy and steadfastness often found on the settings of 16th- and 17th-century jewelry. Henri IV of France made prolific use of the barred S in the portrait miniatures he presented to his mistress, Gabrielle d'Estrées.

Along the same lines is an older and more widespread motif that can also be found in the collection of the Musée des Arts Décoratifs; two clasped hands. It dates back to earliest antiquity (in the teachings of Pythagoras it represented the number ten, the mystical sum of all the other numbers, also symbolized by the triangular shape called the tetractys) and survived until the 19th century, particularly in the Victorian era, when it was commonly used on jewelry and on tombstones. Carved into the bezel of a ring or engraved on the back of a portrait miniature, it served as a sign of enduring romantic or spiritual love, of a fidelity that transcended not only the vicissitudes of desire but also the very limits of life and death: a symbol of loss redeemed by the hope of reunification in the next life.

Figures and faces cannot, therefore, be dissociated from their settings, which often grow more complex as the figures become simplified. This is not only because the setting can make use of a wealth of decorative arabesques, openwork and scrollwork and a rich variety of stones and precious metals, but also because it provides a key to the reading of the portrait, enshrining it and bestowing an almost religious quality upon it. The same quasi-religious connotations can be found in the kind of fetishization or intense focus that strips a portrait down until all that remains of the face is an eye, the window of the soul, gazing directly at the viewer, in a form of fragmentation reminiscent of votive offerings.

This journey concludes with the image of an anonymous and enigmatic eye – recalling the eye of Lord Byron, with its indescribable colours, or the eye shedding a diamond tear, both of which can be found in the collections of the Musée Carnavalet. Despite the brief and necessarily incomplete nature of this survey, it clearly demonstrates that if there is one function shared by the multiple roles played by figurative motifs, it is that of symbolic, religious or intimate celebration. Whether it is political, metaphysical, public, private, familial or romantic, figurative jewelry is always essentially devotional in nature.

Patrick Mauriès

THE BEJEWELED
BODY

'It would be as rare to find the entire human figure in full relief in antique jewelry as it is unseemly in modern jewelry,' the art critic Charles Blanc wrote in 1875. He tolerated the inclusion of figures in cameos or intaglios but rejected it in three-dimensional form: 'whether as a caryatid in an architectural composition or in lifelike motion performing a specific gesture, it completely spoils the jewelry due to the fact that it is no longer on a human scale and because the human body takes on too many forms, is too beautiful, too important, and holds too high a rank in creation to play a supporting role amid images drawn from the world of flora or geometry.' Blanc's anthropocentric view of creation did not allow the human body to be treated as a mere ornament, and he denied jewelry its symbolic significance. He adopted a purely formal stance, refusing to allow artists the freedom to simplify or interpret the human figure and transpose it into a minor art form that he regarded as a mere means of adornment for ladies.

Despite Blanc's misgivings, the representation of the human body is as widespread and as ancient in the art of jewelry as that of other motifs derived from the living world, such as plants and animals. Prehistoric wall paintings depict hunters with their prey. Three-dimensional carvings have been dated to 40,000–35,000 BC. The earliest figure of all, the Venus of Hohle Fels (Swabian Jura, Germany), 6 cm (2½ in.) high, is headless but includes a ring above its shoulders, suggesting that the figure was meant to be hung from a cord. There is no suspension ring on the Venus of Lespugue, whose head is smooth and featureless. The Venus of Brassempouy, also known as the 'Lady with the Hood', is one of the earliest known representations of a human face; her tiny size, only 3.65 cm (1½ in.) in height, suggests that she was meant to be carried as an amulet or keepsake, perhaps in a small leather bag. All of these figures, with their exaggerated female forms, are linked to fertility cults. Some of the stylized figurines found in Dolní Věstonice (Czech Republic), adorned with breasts or male genitals, include suspension rings on the rear. While the presence of a suspension ring shows that objects were worn as pendants, others can be recognized as jewelry only by their small size.

In antiquity, the representation of the human body was linked to the cult of gods, heroes and famous men. In ancient Egypt, the pharaoh was depicted alongside the gods in bas-relief tomb carvings and on jewelry such as necklaces or bracelets. In Mesopotamia, the gods were shown in human form on engraved cylinder seals and relief carvings. The cameos and intaglios of ancient Greece depicted images of gods, goddesses and heroes accompanied by their symbols, or acting out scenes from their lives. Earrings were adorned with figures of Victory or Eros. In Rome, fashionable cameos and intaglios featured the profiles of emperors and empresses, who also appeared on medallions and jewelry, including a ring with a gold bust that belonged to Emperor Marcus Aurelius and dates from the second century AD (Staatliche Antikensammlungen, Munich).

In Byzantium and the medieval West, representations of Christ, the Virgin and the saints on enamelled plaques stood out among the antique intaglios and cameos that were reused because of their colour and beauty. Royal crowns were adorned with the figures of angels, like those on the crown King Louis IX gave to the Dominicans of Liège (Louvre, Paris). Reliquary pendants depicted scenes from the life of Christ in ronde-bosse enamel. In the 15th century, rosary beads could be opened to reveal religious scenes in relief enamel, while brooches and other insignia were adorned with the heads of couples (Kunsthistorisches Museum, Vienna).

The humanist Renaissance embraced the human figure and its representation on jewelry reached an unparalleled degree of excellence during that period. Religious faith was expressed in rosary beads carved from boxwood and filled with scenes from the life of Christ, or shaped from ivory, in the form of skulls with many faces, types of *memento mori* that, as pointed out by Alain Tapié (curator of a 2010 exhibition on the theme of the vanitas entitled *Vanité*), are more than morbid souvenirs: 'Far from just being a symbol of death, it [the skull] signifies going beyond it, towards eternal salvation.' The everyday presence of these motifs was thought to encourage believers to prepare for a good – i.e. Christian – death. Other less sinister pieces depict stories from the Bible, such as Joseph pulled from the pit by his brothers (British Museum, London). Alongside these devotional works, there were secular images of warriors or knights on enamelled cap badges surrounded by diamonds and rubies (Sir John Soane's Museum, London). Baroque pearls were used on pendants and brooches to represent figures of fantasy (mermaids, knights, St George) or mythological characters, such as *Europa and the Bull* (National Gallery of Art, Washington, DC). The jewelers of the time also cast their gazes back to ancient mythology for images of love, in the form of cornelian rings whose bezels could be opened to reveal figures in ronde-bosse enamel.

Draughtsmen and engravers such as Hans Collaert, Jacques Androuet du Cerceau or Étienne Delaune in the 16th century filled their compositions with confronted figures positioned on either side of enamelled or engraved medallions. These male or female figures were sometimes combined with fantastical beings, half-man, half-beast.

Sometimes artists reused antique medallions, but more usually they would design new versions, embellished with inscriptions and mottoes or with portraits of the kings and queens, emperors and empresses of Europe, following in the footsteps of the emperors of ancient Rome. These images of famous men in ronde-bosse enamel (e.g. the insignia of Charles V, Kunsthistorisches Museum, Vienna) or painted enamel (the portrait of James I by Nicholas Hilliard, British Museum, London) herald the development in the 18th century of the painted portrait miniatures that proliferated on pendants and rings until the invention of photography in the mid-19th century. These painted portraits, many of which still survive, could be framed and attached to the wall but they could also be worn, either openly or concealed inside pieces of jewelry, often together with locks of hair. Reflecting a certain sentimentality and the greater importance now bestowed upon family life, these pieces could include images of married couples and children, sometimes in the context of mourning.

In France under the Empire, classical revivals brought a resurgence of cameos and intaglios, both ancient and modern, in parures and diadems, often depicting mythological figures. In the early 19th century, portrait jewelry, whether intimate or political, still remained fashionable, including pieces featuring portraits of Louis XVI, Marie-Antoinette or the royal children worn during the Bourbon Restoration. A legacy from the age of the Revolution, political rings served as a means of showing support or advertising the allegiances of their owner. During the Romantic period, jewelry made references to the fashionable novels and short stories of the time: brooches and châtelaines retold scenes from the Middle Ages, showing noblemen on horseback going hunting with falcons, or knights kneeling at the feet of their lady. The jewelers and goldsmiths of the time worked in close collaboration with engravers. Under the Second Empire, jewelers copied famous portraits in painted enamel or adorned their pieces with reproductions of sculptures in semi-precious stones. Cameo carving attained a level of quality rarely seen before, until giving way, towards the end of the 19th century, to a revival of medallions, which were now easier to reproduce by using a reducing lathe.

At the close of the century, under the Third Republic, and in particular at the Expositions Universelles of 1878 and 1889 in Paris, multiple sources of inspiration from the 19th century were merged with a very strong Renaissance influence, leading to representations of the human figure in gold, enamelwork and gemstones. The jeweled chokers created by Alphonse Fouquet are decorated with painted enamel figures or heads of women in ronde-bosse enamel. Art Nouveau jewelry embraced nymphs and other female nudes, allegories of nature and woman, surrounded by flowers and plants, while other more light-hearted pieces combined floral motifs with faces rendered in matt enamel.

Images of the human figure became rarer in the jewelry of the 20th century, although they can be found in the 1930s on pendants decorated with ritualistic masks derived from African art. It then took until the 1960s for them to reappear, in the form of the mythologically inspired faces created by the artist Georges Braque, or the enigmatic openwork mask motifs of Jean Lurçat. Today's jewelry artists like to represent individual body parts (mouths, fingers) that were formerly only depicted in isolation when associated with superstitious beliefs and protective spiritual practices.

Human figures and faces in jewelry can carry a wide range of meanings, far more so than animal and plant motifs. Whether they express devotion, sentiment or allegiance, figurative jewels bear witness to those who once wore them and to the societies that created them.

Évelyne Possémé

Mythological
FIGURES

Since antiquity, the imaginary lives and loves of gods, goddesses and heroes have inspired artists to depict fantastical figures. Medusa is one of the three Gorgons, divinities whose eyes can turn any mortal who gazes upon them into stone. After she was beheaded by Perseus, her head was given to the goddess Athena who attached it to her shield. The image of Medusa, whether as a bust or a mask, has long been used as a protection against the evil eye. Artists also admired her sculptural qualities: the face of a woman whose hair is intertwined with snakes.

Right and opposite:
Medusa brooch
Naples, 2nd half of 19th century
Gilded silver, lava stone, black enamel
H. 7.5 cm; W. 5 cm
Gift of the widow Mme Meissonier, 1891
Inv. 6992

Heads and busts of female figures from Greek and Roman mythology are well suited to jewelry, especially brooches. Faces in bas-relief or in the round may be sculpted from precious substances, including the ornamental stones used for cameos and intaglios, or from less costly materials such as shell and coral. The cities of Naples and Torre del Greco were major production centres for carved coral, with some designs dating back as far as the 18th century. In the century that followed, Marseille also began to specialize in the carving of these organic materials. Heads of Medusa, nymphs, and bacchantes or maenads are regularly reproduced in this manner, along with their characteristic ornaments. Often portrayed with bunches of grapes in their hair, bacchantes are sometimes also accompanied by putti or, as in the case of this brooch, sea putti carrying conch shells.

Head of a Bacchante brooch
France, Louis-Philippe period (1830–48)
Gold, carved coral
H. 5.5 cm; W. 4.6 cm
Gift of Count Blaise
de Montesquiou-Fezensac, 1927
Inv. 29029

René Lalique (1860–1945)
Siren tiara
Bronze, gold, carved and cabochon opals,
enamel
H. 9.7 cm; W. 14 cm; D. 13.3 cm
Gift of Marquis Hubert de Ganay
in memory of the Countess of Béarn,
née Martine de Béhague, 1939
Inv. 34374

Mythological imagery fell from favour in the Middle Ages but was revived during the Renaissance thanks to the rediscovery of the literature of classical antiquity, such as Ovid's *Metamorphoses*. The inspiration it provided for the artists of that period continued and grew in the 17th and 18th centuries. Used as a pretext for depicting the naked body, mythology in the 18th century began to merge with the kind of courtly iconography that was often found on men's watchcases.

Left:
Charles Le Roy (1709–71),
Paris watchmaker
Diana Bathing watch (reverse and face)
Gold, painted enamel, glass
H. 6.5 cm; Diam. 5 cm
Gift of Jules Audéoud, 1885
Inv. 2526

Opposite:
Jullijen or Jullien, Paris watchmaker
Venus and Cupid watch
18th century
Gold, steel, enamel, glass, ruby
Diam. 4.3 cm
Bequest of Jean Jacques Reubell, 1934
Inv. 30474

Opposite:
Théophile Laumonnier, jeweler
Bacchante brooch
Paris, 1838–49
Gold, malachite cameo
H. 6.7 cm; W. 5.7 cm
Gift of Henri Vever, 1924
Inv. 24322

Above left:
Minerva brooch
France, Empire period (1804–15)
Gold, rose quartz
H. 4.5 cm; W. 4 cm
Gift of Henri Vever, 1924
Inv. 24242

Above right:
Auguste Vaudet (1838–1914), stone carver
Ceres brooch
Paris, 1877
Gold, black enamel, pearls,
cornelian cameo
H. 4.8 cm; W. 4 cm
Gift of Charles Vaudet, 1945
Inv. 35374

Cameos and hardstone intaglios remained fashionable throughout the 19th century. The carving of fine stones, especially opaque or ornamental hardstones, flourished in France during the Empire period. The most commonly chosen stones for this purpose were banded stones such as agate, made up of multiple overlapping layers in different colours. The lower layer – black or brown – was used as a background, while the white upper layer, which was impervious to dye, was turned into a carved design, often representing a face. Bas-reliefs could also be carved from unlayered stones such as malachite, rose quartz or lava stone.

The reversible nature of this unusual cameo, with its dual heads carved from a single onyx stone, is not apparent at first glance. From the Renaissance onwards, artists like Leonardo da Vinci and Hieronymus Bosch were fascinated by faces with monstrous features, portraits twisted by curved mirrors, and compositions that included distortions and anamorphic elements. In the 16th century, Giuseppe Arcimboldo painted several reversible still-lifes of vegetables or fruits that become portrait caricatures when turned upside down. The ring by René Lalique (opposite) harks back to the classical themes often found in his work, and to stone carving, a technique with which he was familiar and which he used to create relief or intaglio motifs on opal, crystal or glass.

Above:
Reversible Faun's head ring
France, 18th century
Gold, agate cameo
Diam. 2.1 cm; H. 1.7 cm; W. 1.3 cm
Gift of Cérette Meyer, 1938
Inv. 34158

Opposite:
René Lalique (1860–1945), jeweler
Medusa ring
Carved and engraved rock crystal
H. 2.8 cm; Diam. 2.5 cm
Bequest of Jean Jacques Reubell, 1934
Inv. 30081

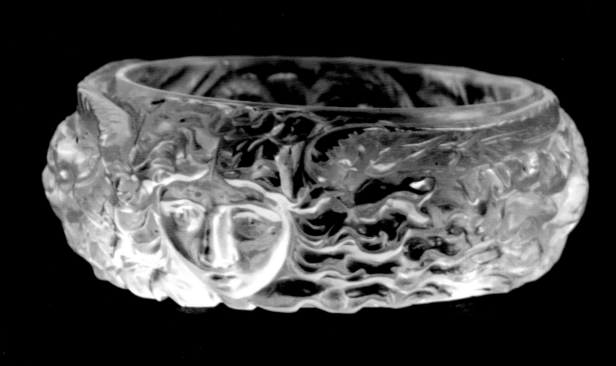

Nature was a primary source of inspiration for Art Nouveau and female figures were a popular subject. Although Art Nouveau plant imagery owed a great deal to the influence of Japanese art, the way the human figure was depicted came directly from the historicism of the 19th century, reworking and updating the Renaissance motifs found in the engravings of Jacques Androuet du Cerceau and Étienne Delaune.

Opposite:
Eugène Grasset (1841–1917), designer
Maison Paul et Henri Vever, jewelers
Omphale necklace
Paris, Exposition Universelle, 1900
Gold, silver, jasper, enamel on gold, rubies, turquoises, opals, cabochon emeralds, brilliant-cut diamonds
L. necklace 29 cm; H. motif 14 cm; W. 12 cm
Gift of Henri Vever, 1924
Inv. 24521

Above right:
François-Désiré
Froment-Meurice (1802–55)
The Toilet of Venus pendant
Paris, c. 1855
Gold, amethyst, enamel, pearls
H. 6 cm; W. 4 cm
Gift of Henri Vever, 1924
Inv. 24471

Below right:
Maison Paul et Henri Vever
Daphnis and Chloe comb
Paris, Exposition Universelle, 1900
Ivory, gold, pearls, translucent openwork enamel
H. 18 cm; W. 4.5 cm
Gift of Henri Vever, 1924
Inv. 24538

Giuseppe Girometti (1780–1851), engraver
Achilles bracelet
Rome and Paris, 1846
Gold, sardonyx cameo,
amethysts, diamond
Bracelet: W. 4.1 cm; L. 19 cm
Medallion: H. 7.2 cm; W. 6 cm
Deposited by the Musée du Louvre, 1944
Inv. LOUVRE OA 9377

Figures of
DEVOTION

Jewelry with religious motifs can be found from the Byzantine era to the present day. Pendants or brooches may act as signs of religious affiliation or personal beliefs. The pendants of the 17th and 18th centuries rework the scholarly symbolism found in great religious paintings, using techniques such as reverse painting or reverse gilding on glass. These two techniques were often utilized in tandem, as in this double-sided, heart-shaped pendant, depicting scenes from the Nativity and the Annunciation. The gold leaf and painted figures have been applied to the underside of a rock crystal plaque.

Right and opposite:
Annunciation and *Nativity*
double-sided pendant
Spain, early 19th century (?)
Gold, reverse painted crystal,
enamel, baroque pearls
H. 8.2 cm; W. 5 cm
Bequest of the widow
of René Ménard, 1969
Inv. 41868

These elaborate beads were used for religious meditation. A few examples survive as part of a decade rosary, made up of ten smaller beads, with one end bearing a crucifix and a ring that could be hung from the finger. Large carved beads such as these would hang from the other end of the rosary and could be opened to reveal scenes from the Bible. These boxwood beads are attributed to the workshop of Adam Dircksz, who worked in Delft, in the Netherlands, in the early 16th century.

Left:
Rosary bead: *Crucifixion*
and *Fainting of the Virgin*
Netherlands, 16th century
Carved boxwood
Diam. 3.5 cm
Bequest of Alexandrine
Louise Grandjean, 1923
Inv. GR 799 A

Opposite:
Rosary bead: *Golgotha*
and *Carrying of the Cross*
Netherlands, 16th century
Inscribed in Latin: 'Levemus corda nostra cummanibus ad D' ('Let us lift up our heart with our hands unto God', Lamentations 3: 41); 'Dolore sicut dolore me attendite et videte si est' ('Behold, and see if there be any sorrow like unto my sorrow', Lamentations 1: 12)
Carved boxwood
Diam. 4.5 cm
Bequest of Alexandrine
Louise Grandjean, 1923
Inv. GR 799 B

The demanding technique of
reverse painting has been known
since antiquity. It consists of
painting a scene in reverse on
a transparent layer of glass or
rock crystal so that it can then
be viewed through the glass
the right way around. On this
double-sided pendant, the
images of the Assumption of
the Virgin and St Francis of
Assisi have been painted on
two separate crystal plaques,
set inside a reversible mount
in chiselled gold.

Right and opposite:
Assumption of the Virgin
and Saint Francis of Assisi
double-sided pendant
Spain, early 18th century (?)
Gold, reverse painting on rock crystal
H. 7 cm; W. 5 cm
Bequest of Marquise
Arconati-Visconti, 1925
Inv. 23982

As accessories for personal and private devotion, rings and rosary beads depicting religious subjects could easily be touched or contemplated by their owner at any time. These portable forms of worship were used from the Byzantine period until the Renaissance. Rings decorated with Crucifixion scenes were particularly popular during the Renaissance. From the 17th century onwards, symbols of devotion became more discreet; simple medallions appeared in the 19th century and continued to be popular throughout the 20th century. Today, some artists have revived religious symbols for the purposes of fashion, particularly crucifixes, distancing them from their religious significance.

Above left:
Virgin and Child ring
Byzantine, 6th–7th century
Nielloed gold, platinum bead
Diam. 2.4 cm; H. 1.6 cm; W. 1.5 cm
Bequest of Jean Jacques Reubell, 1934
Inv. 30097

Above right:
Crucifixion ring
Germany (?), 16th century
Gold, enamel
Diam. 3 cm; H. 2 cm; W. 2 cm
Bequest of Jean Jacques Reubell, 1934
Inv. 30858

Opposite:
Line Vautrin (1913–97)
St Lubin, Breton Saint of Healing brooch
Paris, c. 1945
Gilt bronze, lacquer
H. 6 cm; W. 5 cm
Gift of Yvonne Brunhammer, 1990
Inv. 990.287

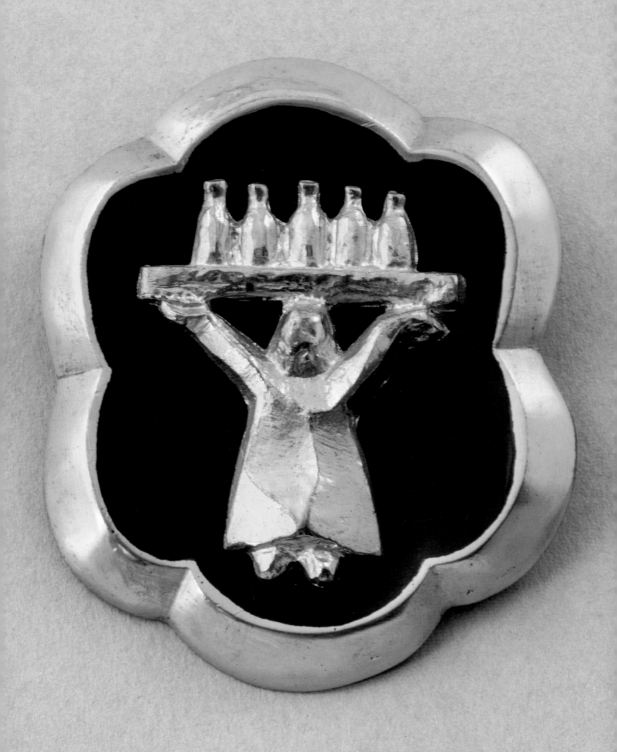

Opposite:
Jacob and the Angel ring
France, 18th century
Gold, rubies, enamel painted
on porcelain
Diam. 2.7 cm; H. 2.1 cm; W. 2.5 cm
Gift of Cérette Meyer, 1938
Inv. 34173

Above:
Virgin and *Saint John the Baptist*
double-sided pendant
France, 15th century
Gilded silver, *basse-taille* enamel on silver
H. 5.5 cm; W. 3.5 cm
Bequest of Charles Pascal Marie Piet-La-
taudrie, 1910
Inv. 16747

Many pieces of jewelry reflect a devotion to particular saints and the lasting popularity of stories from the Old and New Testament. The cult of the Virgin was significant from the Middle Ages onwards and continued to grow in strength until the 19th century, which saw the official definition of the dogma of the Immaculate Conception. The figure of the Virgin could often be identified by her blue cloak, together with flowers such as the lily, a symbol of purity, or the rose. Scenes could be rendered in the form of sculpture, glass painting or painted enamel on porcelain or metal. Transparent *basse-taille* enamels such as the pendant shown above were generally set in a low-relief mount of chiselled gold or silver.

Religiously themed jewelry is sometimes inspired by painful events, such as bereavement. This is the case for the *Calvary* ring made by engraver Jules Brateau in memory of his son, who died in the Great War in 1914 at the age of twenty. The ring's bezel represents a bleeding heart surrounded by a crown of thorns, supported at the shoulders by two angels holding the instruments of the Passion of Christ: one carries the column and two nails, the other the reed and the hammer. On other occasions, the imagery of Catholicism may be reworked in a more oblique fashion, creating costume jewelry in which the choice of non-precious materials reflects an old-fashioned and somewhat kitsch concept of devotion.

Below:
Jules Brateau (1844–1923)
Calvary ring
Paris, c. 1914
Gold, copper, red glass heart
Inscribed: 'In memory of my beloved son
Jean Brateau, Sergeant, 40th Artillery
Regiment, killed on 22 August 1914
in Joppécourt M. and M.' and 'J. Brateau
his father'
H. 3.6 cm; Diam. 2.6 cm
Gift of Philippe Rausch, 2001
Inv. 2002.173.6

Opposite:
Christine Buri-Herscher (born 1935)
Sanctuary necklace
Paris, 1983
Metal, bisque porcelain, glass, plastic
L. 37 cm; W. 14 cm; statuette H. 12.2 cm
Deposited by the Centre National
des Arts Plastiques, Ministère
de la Culture et de la Communication, 1984
Inv. FNAC 2285

Figures of
LOVE

Images of children are frequently found in jewelry but it is often difficult to interpret their religious or mythological meaning. Angels, putti and Cupids: are they merely jolly naked babies or allegories? Whether depicted full length or in bust form, these figures were sometimes chosen simply to represent typical childhood scenes, such as laughter and tears in this pair of earrings. Portraits of children are clearly identifiable on some pieces, often accompanied by allegorical symbols. On other works, they are associated with expressions of love.

Right and opposite:
Eugène Fontenay (1823–87)
Laughing Child and *Crying Child* earrings
Paris, c. 1867
Gold, filigree gold, carved lapis lazuli
H. 7.5 cm; W. 2.5 cm
Gift of Henri Vever, 1924
Inv. 24441

Jewelry often conveys a message of love. The ring shown below, its bezel decorated with a reverse painting on crystal of Cupid carrying two burning hearts on a dish, clearly announces to the world that its wearer is in love and therefore no longer free. The bezel can also be reversed, perhaps to hold a miniature or a lock of the beloved's hair. The scene of a young woman reading a letter, meanwhile, is part of the classic pictorial iconography of love, and is also regularly found on jewelry.

Left:
Cupid ring with swivel bezel
France, late 18th century
Gold, reverse painting on glass
Bezel H. 2 cm; W. 1 cm
Gift of Cérette Meyer
in memory of her brother, 1914
Inv. 19450

Opposite:
The Letter ring
France or England, late 18th century
Partially gilded silver, guilloché enamel
on gold, paste gemstones
H. 4.3 cm; W. 2 cm
Gift of Cérette Meyer
in memory of her brother, 1914
Inv. 19434

Opposite:
Gustave Baugrand (1826–70)
Comedy demi-parure
Paris, 1852–70
Gold, miniatures on porcelain,
enamel, rose-cut diamonds
Brooch: H. 3.7 cm; W. 4 cm
Earrings: H. 6.5 cm; W. 2 cm
Gift of Henri Vever, 1924
Inv. 24434 A and B

Above:
Allegory of Hope reversible pendant
France, early 19th century
Gold, reverse painting on glass,
miniature on ivory
H. 5.5 cm; W. 4.5 cm
Gift of Henri Vever, 1924
Inv. 24238 A

Pairs of semi-nude putti accompany the allegorical personification of Comedy in this demi-parure dating from the second half of the 19th century. Medallions painted on porcelain were often inspired by 18th-century French decorative paintings. Pendants combining a portrait with an allegory of Hope are typical of the early 19th century. This kind of jewelry can be seen in the miniatures that decorated the lids of ornamental boxes during the First Empire: they show fashionably dressed women in high-waisted gowns with short-sleeved bodices, whose low-cut neckline reveals a pendant of this kind, generally hanging from a chain with a heart-shaped clasp.

Discovered in the first half of the 19th century, aluminium was initially regarded as a precious metal, and hence was used in jewelry and fine metalwork. The few known jewelry pieces dating from this period are inspired by rococo motifs, with delicately engraved Cupids and putti, highlighted with different shades of gold. Steel, meanwhile, has been used in jewelry since the 18th century in the form of faceted hemispheres, polished and riveted to mounts made of the same metal. During the 1840s, steel and gold jewelry with geometric motifs became fashionable and jewelers, inspired by the work of medieval goldsmiths, created pieces from damascened steel inlaid with gold and turquoises.

The bezel of this ring represents the head of a putto carved in cornelian. It conceals a hinged lid that opens to reveal a figure in ronde-bosse enamel, representing a Cupid with two-colour wings. The inside of the lid holds the attributes of the god: a quiver, arrows, a torch and a bow tied with a ribbon, surrounded by a garland of foliage. The reverse and shoulders of the bezel are enamelled in black and white. This ring could be regarded as a form of 'secret compartment' jewelry, since the cherub's head on the bezel is scarcely legible and it is not immediately apparent that the iconography relates to love.

Wedding rings may incorporate a range of motifs: a portrait of the couple, a Gordian knot, a crowned heart, clasped hands. The body of the ring may be made up of two interlocking rings. Fede rings, known since the 12th century, are characterized by the motif of two clasped hands. This motif, which dates back to classical Rome, symbolizes the sealing of a contract; its name comes from the Italian *mani in fede,* meaning 'hands joined in faith'. In most cases, the hands form the bezel of the ring but they are sometimes found on the reverse, with the bezel featuring a portrait of the husband or wife. From the 16th century onwards, a variant design featured two hands on either side of a burning heart or two interlocked hearts.

From top to bottom:
Fede ring
Italy (?), 15th century
Nielloed silver
H. 2 cm; W. 2 cm
Bequest of Jean Jacques Reubell, 1934
Inv. 30813

Goldsmith signed VD (?)
Fede ring
Rouen, 1750
Gold
H. 1.1 cm; Diam. 2.2 cm
Bequest of Jean Jacques Reubell, 1934
Inv. 30707

Wedding ring
Germany (?), 17th century (?)
Gold, enamel
H. 1 cm; Diam. 2.2 cm
Bequest of Jean Jacques Reubell, 1934
Inv. 30396

Interlocked wedding ring
Germany (?), 17th century (?)
Gold, enamel, rubies, turquoises
H. 2.3 cm; Diam. 2 cm
Bequest of Jean Jacques Reubell, 1934
Inv. 30597

Jewelers have long preferred allegorical or symbolic representations of love to more explicit depictions. It took until the early 20th century, and the creations of René Lalique, for subjects such as kisses or embracing couples to appear in the iconography of jewelry. The brooch named *The Kiss* is a unique and exceptional piece within Lalique's body of work, and makes use of a technique inspired by cameo and intaglio carving, applied to moulded glass. As with some works by Émile Gallé, Lalique makes this piece itself speak, for it is inscribed with the words 'I dream of kisses that last forever', while the surrounding garland of thorns expresses the duality of love.

Above:
René Lalique (1860–1945)
Dancing Couples ring
Paris, c. 1899–1901
Gold, button pearl
Diam. 2.1 cm; H. 2.6 cm; W. 1.6 cm
Gift of Baroness Félix Oppenheim, 1933
Inv. 28864

Opposite:
René Lalique (1860–1945)
The Kiss brooch
Inscribed: 'I dream of kisses
that will last forever',
poem by Sully Prudhomme (1839–1907)
Paris, c. 1904–6
Patinated silver, moulded glass, enamel
H. 4.9 cm; W. 7 cm
Gift of M. R. C. Le Mesnil, 1960
Inv. 38337

Contemporary jewelry has broken free from the codes and sentimental symbolism of earlier times. Yet some motifs, such as clasping hands, survive in oblique form and can be used to express different kinds of human relationship, whether consciously or not. When placed around the neck, as seen overleaf, the hands may evoke strangling and possession rather than trust. Some works are even more dramatic and daring, such as Florence Lehmann's necklace *Close-Fitting Birth*, representing the end result of physical love: giving birth, another tight squeeze in both real and figurative terms. In this revealing piece, the artist examines the relationship between man and woman, male domination and female alienation.

Florence Lehmann (born 1964)
Strasbourg, 2002–6
Close-Fitting Birth necklace
Painted wood
H. 12 cm; Diam. 36 cm
Deposited by the Centre National
des Arts Plastiques, Ministère
de la Culture et de la Communication, 2012
Inv. FNAC 07-414

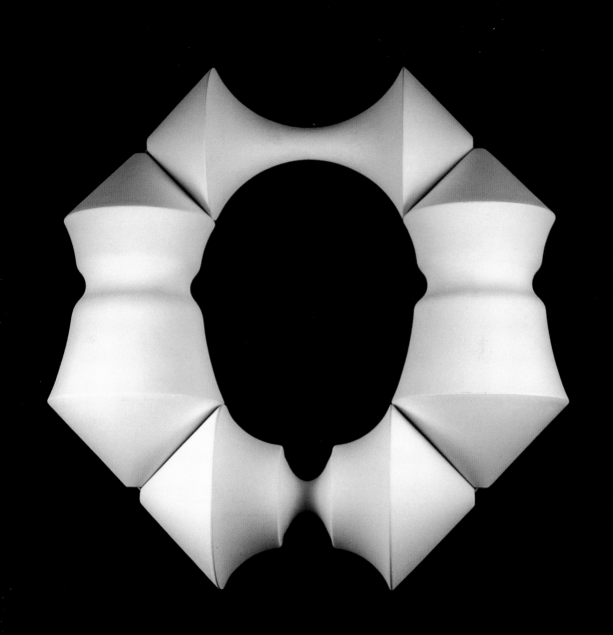

Jacomijn van der Donk (born 1963)
Hands necklace
Netherlands, 1994
Oxidized silver lace
H. 4.5 cm; W. 30 cm
Deposited by the Centre National
des Arts Plastiques, Ministère
de la Culture et de la Communication, 1996
Inv. FNAC 95310

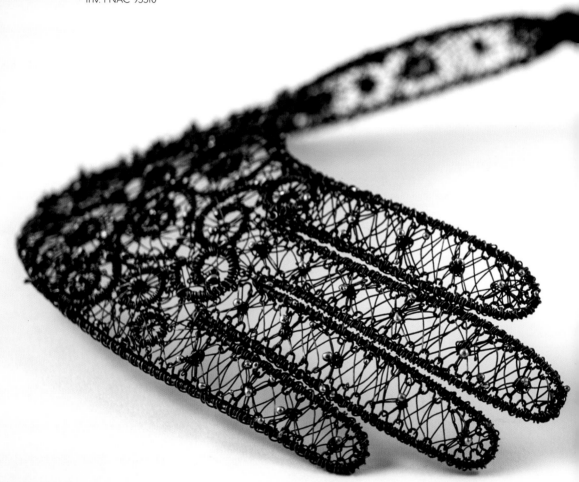

Historical
FACES

In the realm of jewelry, historical references may involve major events or smaller, more personal moments. Depending on the happenings of their own time, jewelers and their clients could be just as interested in the fashions, follies and fictionalized figures of history as in the individuals who shaped contemporary life. This kind of jewelry, therefore, can take on multiple aspects: historical, sentimental, political or simply anecdotal. It can be used to signal a political commitment, or may reflect one era's fascination with the figures of another era, such as Marie-Antoinette during the Second Empire.

Right and opposite:
Portrait of Marie Leszczynska,
Queen of France necklace
Paris, mid-19th century
After the painting of 1748
by Jean-Marc Nattier
Gold, miniature on porcelain,
paste gemstones, velvet
H. 7.5 cm; L. 35 cm
Gift of Marguerite Arquembourg, 1956
Inv. 37907

In the 19th century, at a time of great political change when various French royal families were fighting for power, jewelry could serve as a sign of political allegiance. By sporting the portraits of the Bourbon line, the legitimists showed their support for the brothers of Louis XVI – Louis XVIII and Charles X, followed by the latter's son, the Duc de Berry, assassinated in 1820, and the Duc d'Angoulême, pretender to the throne from 1836 to 1844. Sometimes, jewelry functioned as proof of membership of an inner circle close to the royal family, such as the ring shown opposite, featuring a portrait miniature of the Empress Josephine, after a painting by Jean-Baptiste Isabey.

Above left:
Louis-Antoine d'Artois,
Duc d'Angoulême pendant
France, 1836–44
Gold, miniature on ivory, rock crystal, silk
H. 2.3 cm; Diam. 2 cm
Gift of Henri Vever, 1924
Inv. 24276 C

Above right:
Frederick II of Prussia ring
Germany (?), c. 1780
After a portrait by Anton Graff (1736–1813)
Gold, miniature on ivory, rock crystal
H. 2.5 cm; Diam. 2.5 cm
Bequest of Jean Jacques Reubell, 1934
Inv. 31045

Opposite:
Jean-Baptiste Isabey (1767–1855),
miniaturist
Joséphine de Beauharnais ring
Paris, c. 1805
After a painting by Jean-Baptiste Isabey,
Josephine in Strasbourg in 1805
H. 3 cm; W. 1.5 cm
Gift of Sylvie Nissen, 2013
Inv. 2013.22.1

Revolutionary France saw a boom in jewelry that symbolized support for the movement and its ideals: this included pendants fashioned from stones from the Bastille or decorated with new political symbols, such as Phrygian caps or fasces. Often made from non-precious materials – iron, steel or silver with a few touches of gold – these pieces showcase the heroes and martyrs of the Revolution. Under the Bourbon Restoration, by contrast, it was King Louis XVI, Queen Marie-Antoinette and their children who were elevated to the rank of martyrs to the royal cause.

The late 19th century saw a Renaissance revival in the arts, spurred by the Exposition Internationale of 1883 and the Exposition Universelle of 1889. Goldwork and jewelry were strongly influenced by this new historicizing style. The trend was reflected not only in the choice of motifs and ornaments, but also in the techniques used. Painted enamel was used to reproduce the portraits of Renaissance monarchs by François Clouet, in particular the famous image of Elisabeth of Austria, wife of Charles IX of France.

Left:
Alfred André (1839–1919), enameller
Falconer cap badge
Paris, 1901
Gold, painted enamel
with counter enamel, enamel
Diam. 4 cm
Gift of Marquise Arconati-Visconti
in memory of M. Raoul Duseigneur, 1916
Inv. 20364

Opposite:
Alphonse Fouquet (1828–1911), jeweler
Paul Grandhomme (1851–1944), enameller
Albert-Ernest Carrier-Belleuse (1824–87), sculptor
Eugène Michaut, engraver
Elisabeth of Austria brooch
Paris, Exposition Universelle, 1878
After a portrait
by François Clouet (1520–72)
Gold, silver, painted enamel,
rose-cut diamonds
H. 12 cm; W. 5.5 cm
Gift of Alphonse Fouquet, 1908
Inv. 14851 D

The events of history can also be personalized in allegorical form. On the pendant shown opposite, a female figure is shown recording history by writing on a shield, a history that seems to be largely military, made up of battles, conquests and deaths, to judge by the pile of enemy skulls lying at the woman's feet, topped by a soldier's helmet. This broken cameo, perhaps dating from antiquity, has been completed by a gold bas relief and attached to a gold mount decorated with a fine band of black enamel, a characteristic trait of First Empire jewelry. Some pieces commemorate painful periods in French history, such as the annexation of Alsace-Lorraine by the German Empire, between 1871 and 1919.

The topaz cameo brooch shown opposite reproduces a portrait of Beatrice Cenci (1577–99) from the early 17th century, attributed to Guido Reni. The daughter of a Roman aristocrat with a violent temper, Cenci tried to escape from her father's incestuous abuse and reported him to the authorities, but the judges took a lenient attitude to crimes committed by the nobility. In despair, Beatrice and her family plotted to kill her father, and were subsequently put on trial and sentenced to death despite the protestations of the people of Rome. The fame of Bianca Capello, wife of Francesco I de' Medici, was also due to her tragic fate. She died a few days after her husband, probably of the same arsenic poisoning that killed him. This painted enamel portrait is based on a marble bust made in 1863 by the female sculptor known as Marcello.

Above:
Alphonse Fouquet (1828–1911), jeweler
Paul Grandhomme (1851–1944), enameller
Charles Béranger (1816–53), enameller
Bianca Capello châtelaine
Paris, Exposition Universelle, 1878
After a marble bust of Bianca Capello
(1863) by Marcello
Gold, enamel painted on
mother-of-pearl, rose-cut diamonds
H. 8.5 cm; W. 7 cm
Gift of Alphonse Fouquet, 1908
Inv. 14851 C

Opposite:
Beatrice Cenci brooch
France, Second Empire (1852–70)
After a portrait of Beatrice Cenci attrib-
uted to Guido Reni (1575–1642)
Gold, topaz cameo, enamel
H. 5.5 cm; W. 4.5 cm
Gift of Henri Vever, 1924
Inv. 24418

Personal
PORTRAITS

In the 18th century, portraits on jewelry mostly took the form of miniatures on ivory. The 19th century preferred techniques that were faster and sometimes less costly, such as shell cameo carving, which allowed the subject to be reworked in later years, especially in the case of portraits of children. This bracelet depicts the Duc de Montebello flanked by his four children in the form of carved shell medallions, in a decorative gold setting that is typical of the Empire period.

Below and opposite:
Marshal Jean Lannes (1769–1809),
Duke of Montebello,
and his Children bracelet
Paris, c. 1810
Gold, shell cameos
H. 5 cm; L. 21 cm
Gift of Marie-Anne
Krugier-Poniatowska, 1997
Inv. 996.III.1

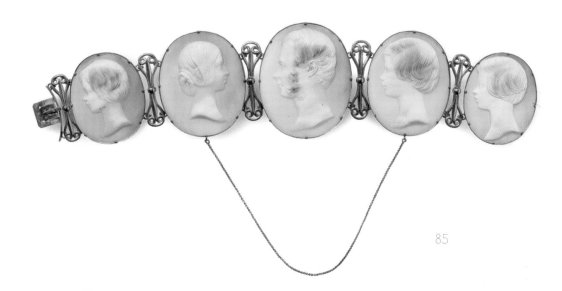

The cameo or intaglio portraits of antiquity were replaced in the 17th century by miniature paintings on ivory. Over the century that followed, portrait jewelry began to reflect the growing importance of the family and children. The philosophers of the Age of Enlightenment, and in particular the writings of Jean-Jacques Rousseau, such as *Emile, or On Education* (1762), emphasized the significance of children to families and married couples. It was no longer considered unseemly to wear or carry an image of one's spouse and children, unlike in previous centuries when such shows of sentiment were frowned upon in high society.

Above left and opposite:
Portrait of a Man and a Woman pendant with reversible medallion
Paris (?), late 18th century
Gilded silver, miniatures on ivory, garnets
H. 5.5 cm; W. 3.5 cm
Bequest of Baroness
Nathaniel de Rothschild, 1901
Inv. 9939

Centre and below left:
Reversible pendant
Italy (?), 16th century
Gilded bronze,
antique chalcedony cameos
H. 5 cm; W. 3 cm
Gift of Jules Maciet, 1887
Inv. 3562

Opposite, above left:
Woman with Blue Veil ring
France (?), late 18th century
Gilded silver and miniature
painted on ivory under glass
H. 2.2 cm; Diam. 2 cm
Bequest of Jean Jacques Reubell, 1934
Inv. 31062

Opposite, right:
Portrait ring
Paris (?), late 18th century
Gold, miniature on ivory, rock crystal
H. 2.7 cm; Diam. 2 cm
Bequest of Jean Jacques Reubell, 1934
Inv. 31046

Opposite, below left:
J. Lecourt, miniaturist at Versailles
Portrait of a Little Girl ring
France, 1804–19
Gold, miniature on ivory, rock crystal
H. 2.3 cm; Diam. 2.1 cm
Gift of Cérette Meyer
in memory of her brother, 1914
Inv. 19453

Above:
Silhouette portrait ring
France, c. 1780
Gold, ivory and tinted ivory, spun glass,
rock crystal, paper
H. 2 cm; W. 2 cm
Gift of Cérette Meyer
in memory of her brother, 1914
Inv. 19448

Rings were often used as settings
for portrait miniatures in the
late 18th century, generally the
face of a child or beloved. In
around 1750, 'shadow portraits'
or silhouettes, named after
Louis XV's controller-general of
finances, Étienne de Silhouette
(1709–67), became fashionable.
These were profiles cut from
black paper, based on the
shadow cast by the subject's
head when lit by candlelight.
In Germany, porcelain
manufacturers sometimes used
silhouette portraits of patrons
in place of the more traditional
coats of arms and monograms.

These busts of women
reproduced in enamel on
watchcases are not portraits but
generic images; most of them
are very similar and represent an
idealized image of womanhood.
Some of these enamels are
enhanced by gemstones
judiciously arranged on the
hats, headdresses or necklines.
The bracelet shown overleaf
was made by François-Désiré
Froment-Meurice for the wife
of the sculptor James Pradier.
It features a shell cameo, based
on a bas-relief created by
Pradier himself, depicting
their three children.

François-Désiré
Froment-Meurice (1802–55), jeweler
Jules Wièse (1818–90), maker
James Pradier (1790–1852), sculptor
Children of James Pradier bracelet
Paris, c. 1841
After a plaster medallion
by James Pradier
Partially gilded silver, shell cameo,
mother-of-pearl, enamel, textile
H. 3 cm; W. 6 cm
Gift of Henri Vever, 1924
Inv. 24383

Figures of
FANTASY

Fantastical figures appeared in
jewelry of the late 19th century
with the advent of Art Nouveau.
This particular stylistic trend
of representing nature in a
heightened and humanized form
continued into the 20th century,
with painters and sculptors
incorporating their ideas into
jewelry. Alberto Giacometti
made several pieces in this
style for the fashion designer
Elsa Schiaparelli, including this
bracelet with the mask of a
naiad, which recalls the lamps
adorned with female faces
that Giacometti created
for the interior designer
Jean-Michel Frank.

Right and opposite:
Alberto Giacometti (1901–66), sculptor
Face of a Chimera or *Naiad* bracelet
Paris, c. 1935
Gilded bronze
Diam. 8 cm
Gift of M. Jean-Yves Mock
in memory of Erica Brausen, 2010
Inv. 2010.27.1

In European art, African figures were originally associated with the allegorical representations of the four continents that first appeared in the 16th century and then became popular additions to the iconography of chateaux and gardens during the 17th century, in particular Versailles under Louis XIV. The figures used to represent Africa were known as 'Moors', a term used in Roman times to designate the Berbers of North Africa and later expanded to refer more broadly to Muslims or to anyone with dark skin. The theme was revived in some 19th-century jewelry, which combined black African figures or faces with feather headdresses of the kind worn by Native Americans, thus demonstrating a lack of knowledge about the motif's original sources.

Above:
Moors earrings
Germany (?), 19th century
Gold, enamel
H. 2 cm; W. 0.9 cm
Bequest of Jean Jacques Reubell, 1934
Inv. 30716 B

Opposite:
Moors earrings
Germany, 18th century (?)
Partially gilded silver, gold, rubies, emeralds, rose-cut diamonds
H. 5 cm; W. 1 cm
Bequest of Baroness
Nathaniel de Rothschild, 1901
Inv. 9859 A and B

The quest for newness that gave rise to Art Nouveau had its roots in the rediscovery of techniques such as enamelling, in the decorative arts of the Middle Ages and the Renaissance, and also in the art of East Asian cultures. Art Nouveau jewelry owed its portrayals of female figures to Renaissance printmakers, its enamel work to traditional French craftsmanship and the art of Chinese cloisonnerie, and its floral and animal motifs to the Japanese art that was first seen in Western Europe in the second half of the 19th century. Art Nouveau designers depicted a stylized realm of the imagination, in which woman represented the link between man and nature.

Opposite:
René Lalique (1860–1945)
Brooch
Paris, c. 1898–99
Gold, enamel on gold, pearl, limestone
H. 6.2 cm; W. 4.5 cm
Bequest of Marquise Arconati-Visconti
in memory of M. Raoul Duseigneur, 1916
Inv. 20371

Overleaf:
René Lalique (1860–1945)
Woman with Poppies pendant and chain
Paris, c. 1898–99
Gold, chalcedony, enamel on gold,
'pearlized' enamel, hollow pearls
H. 10.2 cm; W. 5.7 cm
Gift of Baroness Félix Oppenheim, 1933
Inv. 28867 A

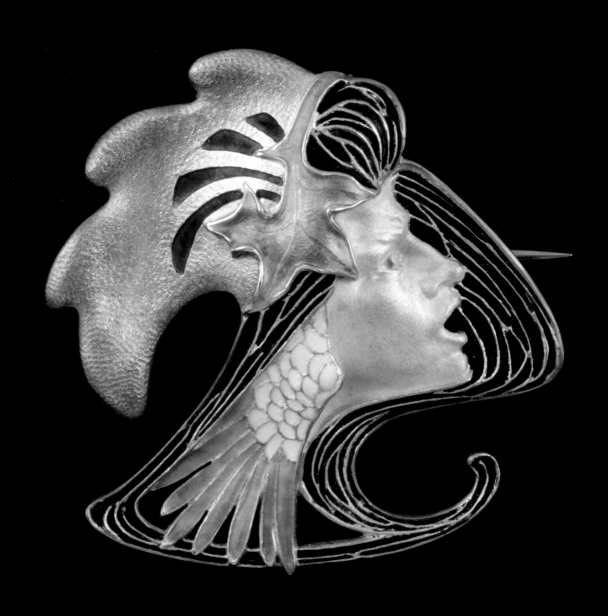

In the era of Symbolism and the pantheistic poetry of writers such as Henri de Régnier, the Art Nouveau style combined the faces and bodies of women with flowers, plants, trees and animals, often depicted in the form of feathered headdresses or bird-like crests. The faces were sometimes rendered in flesh-coloured hardstones, but could also be made of gold coated in matt enamel, a speciality of Georges Le Turcq's work for the Maison Vever.

Elephant ivory has been a sought-after material since the days of antiquity. Because of its colour and the patina it acquires with age, it was once a favourite medium for depictions of the human body, and artists such as René Lalique and Georges Fouquet used it to represent women's bodies or faces. During the Art Deco period, ivory was used to add a touch of white to the multicoloured works shown at the International Exhibition of Modern Decorative and Industrial Arts held in Paris in 1925, before becoming one of the dominant materials at the International Colonial Exhibition in 1931.

The discovery of African art in the early 20th century was a revelation for Western artists working in the fields of the fine and decorative arts. In the 1920s and 1930s, painters and sculptors worked with goldsmiths and jewelry-makers and introduced them to their sources of inspiration. In this way, African and Asian masks became popular jewelry motifs, their ritualistic, introspective and mysterious connotations imbuing the pieces with a new spiritual dimension. The *Ballerina* series by Van Cleef & Arpels was introduced by the house's New York atelier in 1940, followed by its Paris atelier in 1942. The graceful poses of the dancers were designed to show off their golden skirts, set with precious stones, resembling a little girl's dream made real.

Above left:
Pablo Picasso (1881–1973)
Atelier Madoura
Necklace with three medallions
Vallauris, 1949
Terracotta, cotton
Diam. 5 cm
Gift of Mme Karin Cazelles
in memory of Marie-Odile Dussour, 2016
Inv. 2016.149.1

Above right:
Gustave Miklos (1888–1967), sculptor
Raymond Templier (1891–1968), jeweler
Clip
Paris, 1937 and 1942
Silver and silver gilt
Purchased with the support
of the Comité Stratégique, 2010
Inv. 2010.2.1

Opposite:
Van Cleef & Arpels
Ballerina clip
Paris, 1946
Gold, sapphires, brilliant-cut diamonds
H. 2 cm; W. 3.5 cm
Gift of Van Cleef & Arpels, 2017
Inv. 2017.176.1

Jean Lurçat (1892–1966), sculptor
Gilbert Albert (born 1930), jeweler
For Maison Patek Philippe
Mask brooch
Switzerland, 1960–66
Gold
H. 4.5 cm; W. 7.3 cm
Gift of Mme Jean Lurçat, 2003
Inv. 2003.125.12

Parts of the human body have
been reproduced in jewelry
since antiquity for ritualistic
or protective purposes, such
as the votive body parts found
in Greek and Roman places of
worship. Over the centuries,
hands and hearts became
common motifs for sentimental
jewelry. In the 20th century,
some artist-jewelers also became
interested in other body parts,
such as the fingers or mouth.
In 1936 Salvador Dalí created
the famous Mae West Lips
Sofa, with its voluptuous and
provocative curves, in homage
to the Hollywood actress. He
also designed a Lips brooch,
rendered in gold, rubies and
pearls by jewelry-maker Henryk
Kaston; more recently, artists
such as Claude Lalanne and
Solange Azagury-Partridge
have reworked the same motif.

Above:
Solange Azagury-Partridge (born 1961)
Maison Boucheron
Ring, *Eau à la bouche* collection
Paris, 2003
Gold, garnets
Diam. 2.5 cm
Gift of Maison Boucheron, 2004
Inv. 2004.27.6

Opposite:
Claude Lalanne (born 1925)
Mouth necklace
France, 1977
Gilded bronze
Diam. 14.5 cm; H. 4.5 cm; W. 7.5 cm
Gift of Sao Schlumberger, 1996
Inv. 996.115.1

The Art of
THE VANITAS

A traditional Catholic rosary is
made up of beads called aves,
after the prayer *Ave Maria*,
arranged in sets of ten known as
decades. Each decade is followed
by a larger bead known as a
pater or paternoster, in reference
to the Lord's Prayer. Rosaries
with five decades appeared in
the 13th century and later took
on different forms depending on
the number of prayers recited.
In the 19th century, ivory
paternoster beads carved with
heads (skulls, the head of Christ,
male or female faces) were often
separated from their original
rosaries and collected as *memento
mori*. This example, adorned with
red silk tassels, was the terminal
ornament of a single-decade
rosary.

Right and opposite:
Paternoster bead
France (?), 16th century
Ivory, silk
H. 3.5 cm; W. 3.5 cm
Bequest of Baroness
Henri de Rothschild, 1927
Inv. 25650

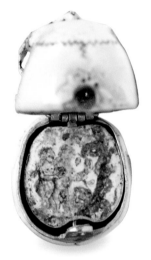

This pendant in the shape of an enamelled gold skull serves as a *memento mori,* but it is also a pomander, used to hold sweet-smelling substances such as ambergris, cinnamon, citronella or rosemary. Within it are four compartments, hidden on each side beneath an enamelled lid. One lid is decorated with polychrome flowers, a motif typical of the first half of the 17th century, inspired by the Ottoman ceramics of Iznik. The other lid is adorned with a scene showing Adam and Eve by the Tree of Knowledge, along with the serpent. The shape and iconography of this striking piece perfectly reflect its dual purpose.

Left and opposite:
Skull pomander
France, 1st half of 17th century
Gold, enamel, rose-cut diamonds
H. 2 cm; W. 1.8 cm; D. 2.3 cm
Bequest of Baroness
Henri de Rothschild, 1927
Inv. 25773

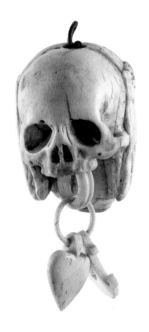

Rings decorated with a skull-and-crossbones motif were common in the 17th and 18th centuries. They served as aids to prayer and meditation, in a similar manner to rosary beads. According to Christian theology, the theological virtues must guide humanity in its relationship with the world and God. These three virtues are Faith, represented by a cross, Hope, represented by an anchor, and Charity, represented by a burning heart. Those three symbols were often hung from rosary beads and, under the Bourbon Restoration in the 19th century, featured on enamelled rings.

Memento mori are aids to meditation and prayer, designed to remind Catholics and Protestants of the ephemeral nature of human life and also of the importance of God and salvation. As well as rosary beads, pendants and rings, skulls also gave their shape to gentlemen's watchcases. This link between the motifs of time and death echoes the hourglasses and watches that were often depicted in the vanitas paintings of northern Europe in the 18th century. The objects included in these pictures – skulls, watches, flowers – were symbols of life, death and the inexorable passage of time.

Above and opposite:
Michel Hechet, watchmaker
Skull watchcase
Watch: Rome, 17th century
Case: France, 17th or early 18th century (?)
Silver
H. 3.5 cm; W. 3.5 cm; D. 4.5 cm
Bequest of Baroness
Henri de Rothschild, 1927
Inv. 25621

Opposite, left:
Skull charm
France, after 1865
Gold, enamel, rose-cut diamonds
H. 2.6 cm; W. 1.4 cm; D. 2.6 cm
Bequest of Baroness
Henri de Rothschild, 1927
Inv. 25774

Opposite, right:
Skull charm
France, after 1865
Gold, enamel, rose-cut diamonds
H. 2.4 cm; W. 1.1 cm; D. 1.3 cm
Bequest of Baroness
Henri de Rothschild, 1927
Inv. 25775

Below:
Skull and Crossbones tie pin
England (?), 19th century
Gold, ivory, enamel, cabochon rubies,
rose-cut diamonds
H. 6 cm; W. 1.5 cm
Bequest of Baroness
Henri de Rothschild, 1927
Inv. 25783

Viewed as a thrilling novelty by some 19th-century writers, electric jewelry featured motifs such as a rabbit playing a drum, a silver skull with ruby eyes and chattering jaws, a quivering butterfly or a bird beating its wings. Worn as a tie pin or on a jacket lapel, the skulls shown opposite were attached to a battery carried discreetly in the wearer's pocket. The mechanism was invented by Gustave Trouvé (1839–1902), a watchmaker and engineer by training, who was interested in the applications of electricity. From 1865 onwards, he began to adapt it to jewelry and presented a selection of pieces at the 1867 Exposition Universelle in Paris, designed in collaboration with the jeweler Auguste-Germain Cadet-Picard.

The collection of skull jewelry bequeathed by Baroness Henri de Rothschild to the Musée des Arts Décoratifs in 1927 reflects the craze known as 'bricabracomania', a fashion for obsessively collecting a huge range of objects of varying quality from many different periods. Skeleton imagery, on objects both ancient or modern, was a subject of widespread interest from the mid-19th century onwards, as Charles Baudelaire noted at the 1859 Salon. The fascination with death, which was no longer religious in overtone, was a sign of the existential malaise depicted and described by late 19th-century artists and thinkers, traces of which can also be found in Symbolist paintings and in practices such as spiritualism.

Above:
Skull and Crossbones ring bezel, mounted on a bracelet
France (?), late 18th–early 19th century
Inscribed in Hebrew: 'For when he dieth he shall carry nothing away; his glory shall not descend after him'
(Psalms 49: 17)
Gold, rock crystal, paper, ink
H. 2.5 cm; W. 2 cm
Bequest of Baroness
Henri de Rothschild, 1927
Inv. 25768

Opposite:
Skull tie pin
Paris, late 19th century
Gold, enamel, rose-cut diamonds
H. 10 cm; W. 1.3 cm; D. 2.4 cm
Bequest of Baroness
Henri de Rothschild, 1927
Inv. 25784

Skull paternoster bead
France, 17th century (?)
Rock crystal, silk
Total H. 19.5 cm;
skull H. 4 cm; W. 3.3 cm; D. 4.1 cm
Bequest of Baroness
Henri de Rothschild, 1927
Inv. 25645

SELECTED BIBLIOGRAPHY

Françoise d'Issembourg d'Happoncourt de Graffigny, *Vie privée de Voltaire et Madame du Châtelet, pendant un séjour de six mois à Cirey*, Paris: Treuttel & Wurtz, 1820

Charles Blanc, *Art in Ornament and Dress* (1875), New York: Scribner, Welford, and Armstrong, 1877

Henri Vever, *French Jewelry of the 19th Century* (1906–8), London: Thames & Hudson, 2001

Guido Gregorietti, *Jewelry Through the Ages*, New York: Simon & Schuster, 1969

J. Anderson Black, *A History of Jewels*, London: Orbis Books, 1974

Jean Lanllier and Marie-Anne Pini, *Five Centuries of Jewelry in the West*, New York: Leon Amiel, 1983

Barbara Cartlidge, *Twentieth-Century Jewelry*, New York: Harry N. Abrams, 1985

Hugh Tait, *Seven Thousand Years of Jewellery*, London: British Museum, 1986

Robin Jaffee Frank, *Love and Loss: American Portrait and Mourning Miniatures*, New Haven, NJ: Yale University Press, 2000

Diana Scarisbrick and James Fenton, *Rings: Jewelry of Power, Love and Loyalty*, London: Thames & Hudson, 2007

Diana Scarisbrick, *Le Grand Frisson. Bijoux de sentiment de la Renaissance à nos jours*, Paris: Textuel, 2008

Alain Tapié, *Vanité. Mort, que me veux-tu*, exhibition catalogue, Paris: Fondation Pierre Bergé-Yves Saint Laurent; Paris: Éditions de La Martinière, 2010

Small Wonders: Late-Gothic Boxwood Micro-Carvings from the Low Countries, exhibition catalogue, Toronto: Art Gallery of Ontario; New York: The Metropolitan Museum of Art; Amsterdam: Rijksmuseum, 2017

Stephen Perkinson, *The Ivory Mirror. The Art of Mortality in Renaissance Europe*, exhibition catalogue, Brunswick, ME: Bowdoin College Museum of Art; New Haven, NJ: Yale University Press, 2017

Above:
Eye pendant
France, late 18th century
Gold, miniature on ivory, glass, hair, silk
H. 5.3 cm; Diam. 4.3 cm
Gift of Marguerite Arquembourg, 1956
Inv. 37887

Overleaf:
Monika Brugger (born 1958)
Borrowed Fingerprints thimbles
France, 2003
Silver
1: H. 2.5 cm; Diam. 1.8 cm
2: H. 2.8 cm; Diam. 2 cm
Deposited by the Centre
National des Arts Plastiques,
Ministère de la Culture
et de la Communication, 2006
Inv. FNAC 05-668.1 and 2

Translated from the French Figures by Francisca Garvie
Photographs by Jean-Marie del Moral
except pages 32 above, 36, 43, 44, 47, 51, 52, 55,
66, 73, 78, 82, 85, 95, 103, 106, 113, 114, 121 (photographs by Jean Tholance)

First published in the United Kingdom in 2018 by
Thames & Hudson Ltd, 181A High Holborn, London WC1V 7QX

www.thamesandhudson.com

First published in the United States of America in 2018 by
Thames & Hudson Inc., 500 Fifth Avenue, New York, New York 10110

www.thamesandhudsonusa.com

British Library Cataloguing-in-Publication Data
A catalogue record for this book is available from the British Library

Library of Congress Control Number 2017959225

ISBN: 978-0-500-02181-1

Printed in Italy